RetailED's Retail Start-Up Workbook

Laura De La Cruz

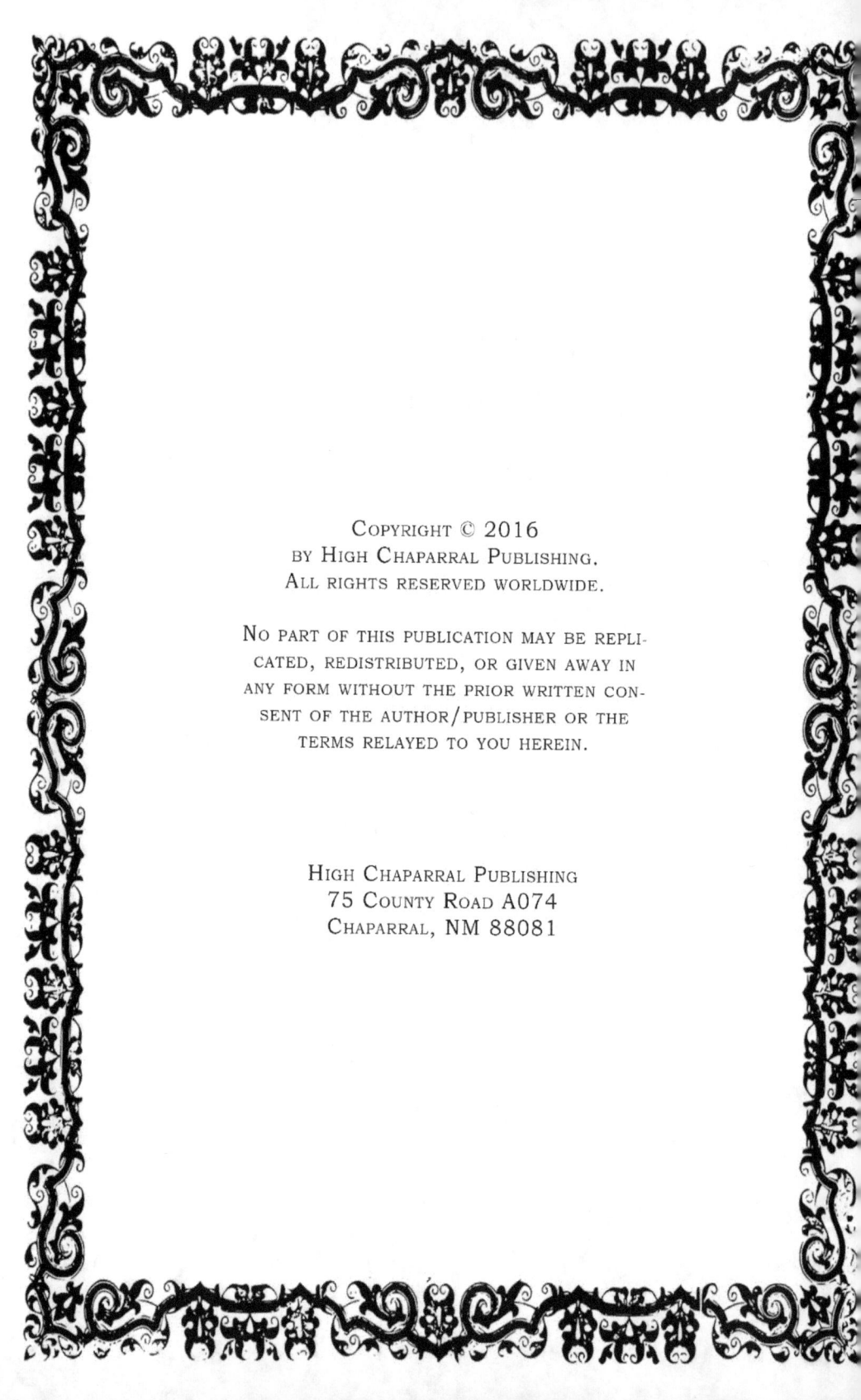

HIGH CHAPARRAL PUBLISHING
75 COUNTY ROAD A074
CHAPARRAL, NM 88081

Retail Business Idea
(What's my niche)

1._____

_____

2._____

_____

3._____

_____

4._____

_____

5._____

_____

Retail Business Idea
(What's my niche)

1._____

_____

2._____

_____

3._____

_____

4._____

_____

5._____

_____

Retail Business Idea
(What's my niche)

1._____

_____

2._____

_____

3._____

_____

4._____

_____

5._____

_____

NOTES

Business Options
(Franchise, Purchase Existing, Etc.)

1._____
_____

2._____
_____

3._____
_____

4._____
_____

5._____
_____

Business Options (Franchise, Purchase Existing, Etc.)

1._____

_____

2._____

_____

3._____

_____

4._____

_____

5._____

_____

Business Options
(Franchise, Purchase Existing, Etc.)

1._____
_____

2._____
_____

3._____
_____

4._____
_____

5._____
_____

NOTES

Business Name Ideas

1. _____
   _____

2. _____
   _____

3. _____
   _____

4. _____
   _____

5. _____
   _____

Business Name Ideas

1._____

_____

2._____

_____

3._____

_____

4._____

_____

5._____

_____

Business Name Ideas

1._____

_____

2._____

_____

3._____

_____

4._____

_____

5._____

_____

NOTES

Products I'll Sell

1._____
_____

2._____
_____

3._____
_____

4._____
_____

5._____
_____

Products I'll Sell

1. _____
   _____

2. _____
   _____

3. _____
   _____

4. _____
   _____

5. _____
   _____

Products I'll Sell

1._____
_____
2._____
_____
3._____
_____
4._____
_____
5._____
_____

NOTES

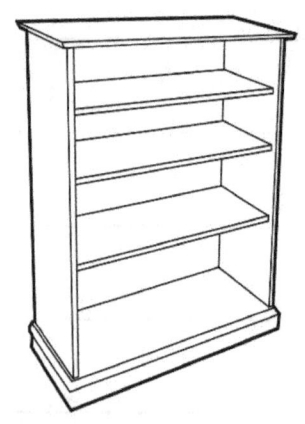

Product Demand Research (Who Wants What I'll Sell)

1._____

_____

2._____

_____

3._____

_____

4._____

_____

5._____

_____

Product Demand Research (Who Wants What I'll Sell)

1._____

_____

2._____

_____

3._____

_____

4._____

_____

5._____

_____

Product Demand Research (Who Wants What I'll Sell)

1._____

_____

2._____

_____

3._____

_____

4._____

_____

5._____

_____

NOTES

Start-Up Costs (An Estimate Of Expenses)

1._____

_____

2._____

_____

3._____

_____

4._____

_____

5._____

_____

Start-Up Costs (An Estimate Of Expenses)

1._____

_____

2._____

_____

3._____

_____

4._____

_____

5._____

_____

Start-Up Costs (An Estimate Of Expenses)

1._____

_____

2._____

_____

3._____

_____

4._____

_____

5._____

_____

NOTES

Who Is My Competition

1._____

_____

2._____

_____

3._____

_____

4._____

_____

5._____

_____

Who Is My Competition

1._____
_____
2._____
_____
3._____
_____
4._____
_____
5._____
_____

Who Is My Competition

1._____

_____

2._____

_____

3._____

_____

4._____

_____

5._____

_____

NOTES

Laws (Local, State & National) I Need To Know About

1._____
_____

2._____
_____

3._____
_____

4._____
_____

5._____
_____

Laws (Local, State & National) I Need To Know About

1._____

_____

2._____

_____

3._____

_____

4._____

_____

5._____

_____

Laws (Local, State & National) I Need To Know About

1._____

_____

2._____

_____

3._____

_____

4._____

_____

5._____

_____

NOTES

Register Business
(When, Where, Registration Numbers)

1._____

_____

2._____

_____

3._____

_____

4._____

_____

5._____

_____

Register Business
(When, Where, Registration Numbers)

1._____
_____

2._____
_____

3._____
_____

4._____
_____

5._____
_____

Register Business
(When, Where,
Registration Numbers)

1._____

_____

2._____

_____

3._____

_____

4._____

_____

5._____

_____

NOTES

Location Ideas

1. _____

_____

2. _____

_____

3. _____

_____

4. _____

_____

5. _____

_____

Location Ideas

1._____

_____

2._____

_____

3._____

_____

4._____

_____

5._____

_____

Location Ideas

1._____
_____

2._____
_____

3._____
_____

4._____
_____

5._____
_____

NOTES

Equipment Needs

1._____

_____

2._____

_____

3._____

_____

4._____

_____

5._____

_____

Equipment Needs

1._____

_____

2._____

_____

3._____

_____

4._____

_____

5._____

_____

Equipment Needs

1._____
_____

2._____
_____

3._____
_____

4._____
_____

5._____
_____

NOTES

Thoughts On
Organizational Structure

1._____
_____

2._____
_____

3._____
_____

4._____
_____

5._____
_____

Thoughts On
Organizational Structure

1._____

_____

2._____

_____

3._____

_____

4._____

_____

5._____

_____

Thoughts On Organizational Structure

1._____

_____

2._____

_____

3._____

_____

4._____

_____

5._____

_____

NOTES

Financing Sources

1._____

_____

2._____

_____

3._____

_____

4._____

_____

5._____

_____

Financing Sources

1._____

_____

2._____

_____

3._____

_____

4._____

_____

5._____

_____

Financing Sources

1._____

_____

2._____

_____

3._____

_____

4._____

_____

5._____

_____

NOTES

Suppliers I May Use

1._____

_____

2._____

_____

3._____

_____

4._____

_____

5._____

_____

Suppliers I May Use

1._____
_____

2._____
_____

3._____
_____

4._____
_____

5._____
_____

Suppliers I May Use

1._____

_____

2._____

_____

3._____

_____

4._____

_____

5._____

_____

NOTES

Store Policies

1._____

_____

2._____

_____

3._____

_____

4._____

_____

5._____

_____

Store Policies

1._____

_____

2._____

_____

3._____

_____

4._____

_____

5._____

_____

Store Policies

1._____

_____

2._____

_____

3._____

_____

4._____

_____

5._____

_____

NOTES

Tradeshows To Attend

1._____

_____

2._____

_____

3._____

_____

4._____

_____

5._____

_____

Tradeshows To Attend

1._____

_____

2._____

_____

3._____

_____

4._____

_____

5._____

_____

Tradeshows To Attend

1._____

_____

2._____

_____

3._____

_____

4._____

_____

5._____

_____

NOTES

Marketing Ideas

1._____
_____

2._____
_____

3._____
_____

4._____
_____

5._____
_____

Marketing Ideas

1._____

_____

2._____

_____

3._____

_____

4._____

_____

5._____

_____

Marketing Ideas

1._____

_____

2._____

_____

3._____

_____

4._____

_____

5._____

_____

NOTES

Social Media

1._____

_____

2._____

_____

3._____

_____

4._____

_____

5._____

_____

Social Media

1._____

_____

2._____

_____

3._____

_____

4._____

_____

5._____

_____

Social Media

1._____

_____

2._____

_____

3._____

_____

4._____

_____

5._____

_____

NOTES

Online Options

1. _____
   _____

2. _____
   _____

3. _____
   _____

4. _____
   _____

5. _____
   _____

Online Options

1._____

_____

2._____

_____

3._____

_____

4._____

_____

5._____

_____

Online Options

1._____
_____

2._____
_____

3._____
_____

4._____
_____

5._____
_____

NOTES

Consultants (Attorney, Accountant, Etc.)

1._____
_____

2._____
_____

3._____
_____

4._____
_____

5._____
_____

Consultants (Attorney, Accountant, Etc.)

1._____

_____

2._____

_____

3._____

_____

4._____

_____

5._____

_____

Consultants (Attorney, Accountant, Etc.)

1._____

_____

2._____

_____

3._____

_____

4._____

_____

5._____

_____

NOTES

Thoughts on Hiring Employees

1._____
_____

2._____
_____

3._____
_____

4._____
_____

5._____
_____

Thoughts on Hiring Employees

1._____

_____

2._____

_____

3._____

_____

4._____

_____

5._____

_____

Thoughts on Hiring Employees

1._____

_____

2._____

_____

3._____

_____

4._____

_____

5._____

_____

NOTES

Business Plan Elements
(A Brief Summary)

1._____

_____

2._____

_____

3._____

_____

4._____

_____

5._____

_____

Business Plan Elements
(A Brief Summary)

1._____

_____

2._____

_____

3._____

_____

4._____

_____

5._____

_____

Business Plan Elements
(A Brief Summary)

1._____
_____

2._____
_____

3._____
_____

4._____
_____

5._____
_____

THANK YOU FOR PURCHASING THIS JOURNAL.
IF YOU ENJOYED IT (OR FOUND SOME USE)
PLEASE LEAVE A POSITIVE REVIEW ON AMAZON.

PLEASE SHARE YOUR RETAIL EXPERIENCES WITH
ME (AND SUGGESTIONS FOR ADDITIONAL WORK-
BOOKS) AT LAURADEL@NMSU.EDU

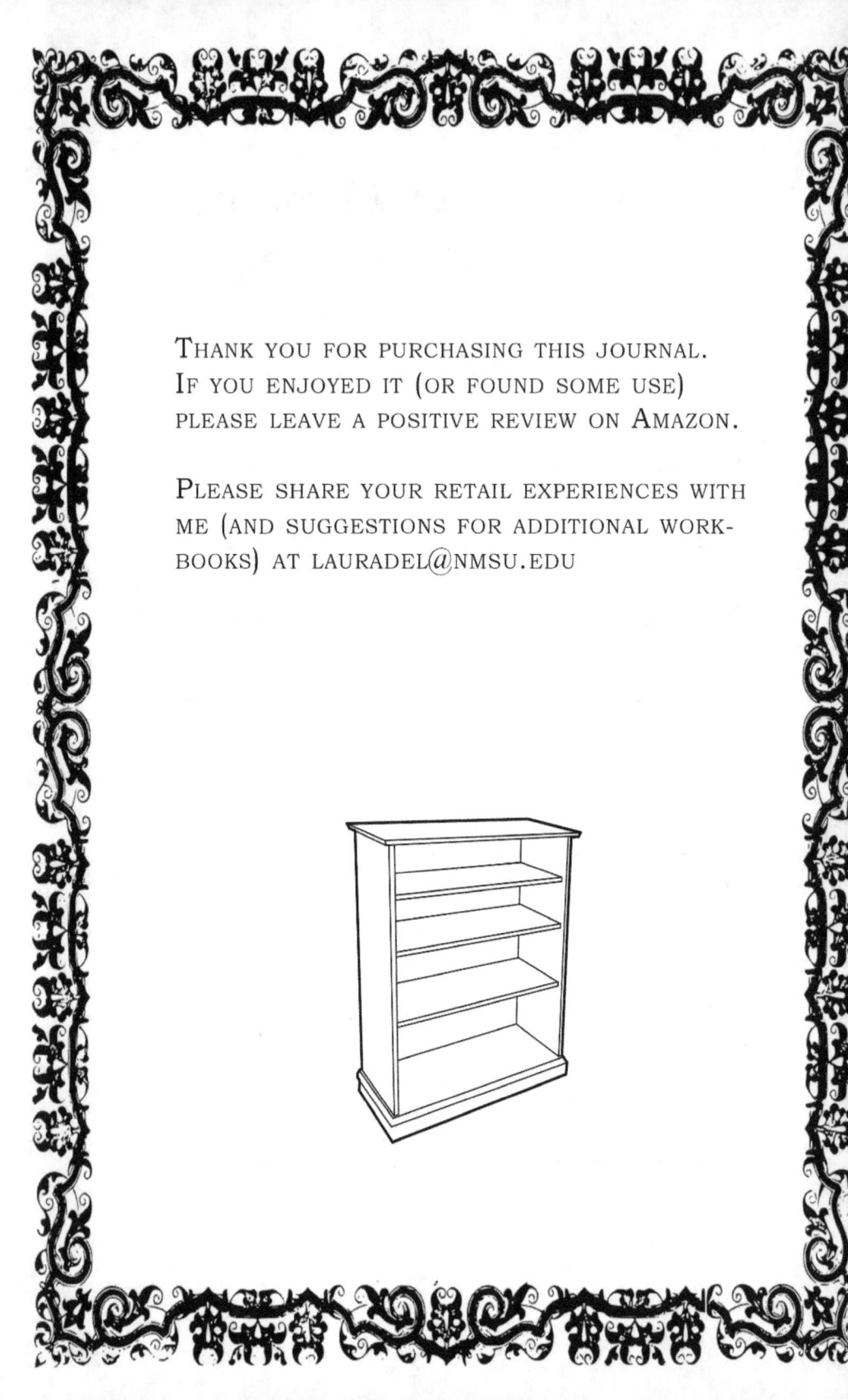

www.ingramcontent.com/pod-product-compliance
Lightning Source LLC
Chambersburg PA
CBHW060405190526
45169CB00002B/764